God Loves Trees

Author: William J. Vanarthos

Editor: William J. Vanarthos

Cover Design: Olivia G. Cianca

All Scripture verses are taken from the New American Standard translation of the Bible unless otherwise specified.

BIASC Classification Suggestions:

1. JNF037040 JUVENILE NONFICTION / Science & Nature / Trees & Forests
2. JNF049200 JUVENILE NONFICTION / Religious / Christian / Early Readers
3. JNF049280 JUVENILE NONFICTION / Religious / Christian / Science & Nature

Paperback ISBN-13: 978-1-937355-94-4

eBook ISBN-13: 978-1-937355-99-9

This book is dedicated to every child, born and unborn, created in the image of God, fearfully and wonderfully made.

> But Jesus called for them, saying, "Permit the children to come to Me, and do not hinder them, for the kingdom of God belongs to such as these."
>
> \- Luke 18:16

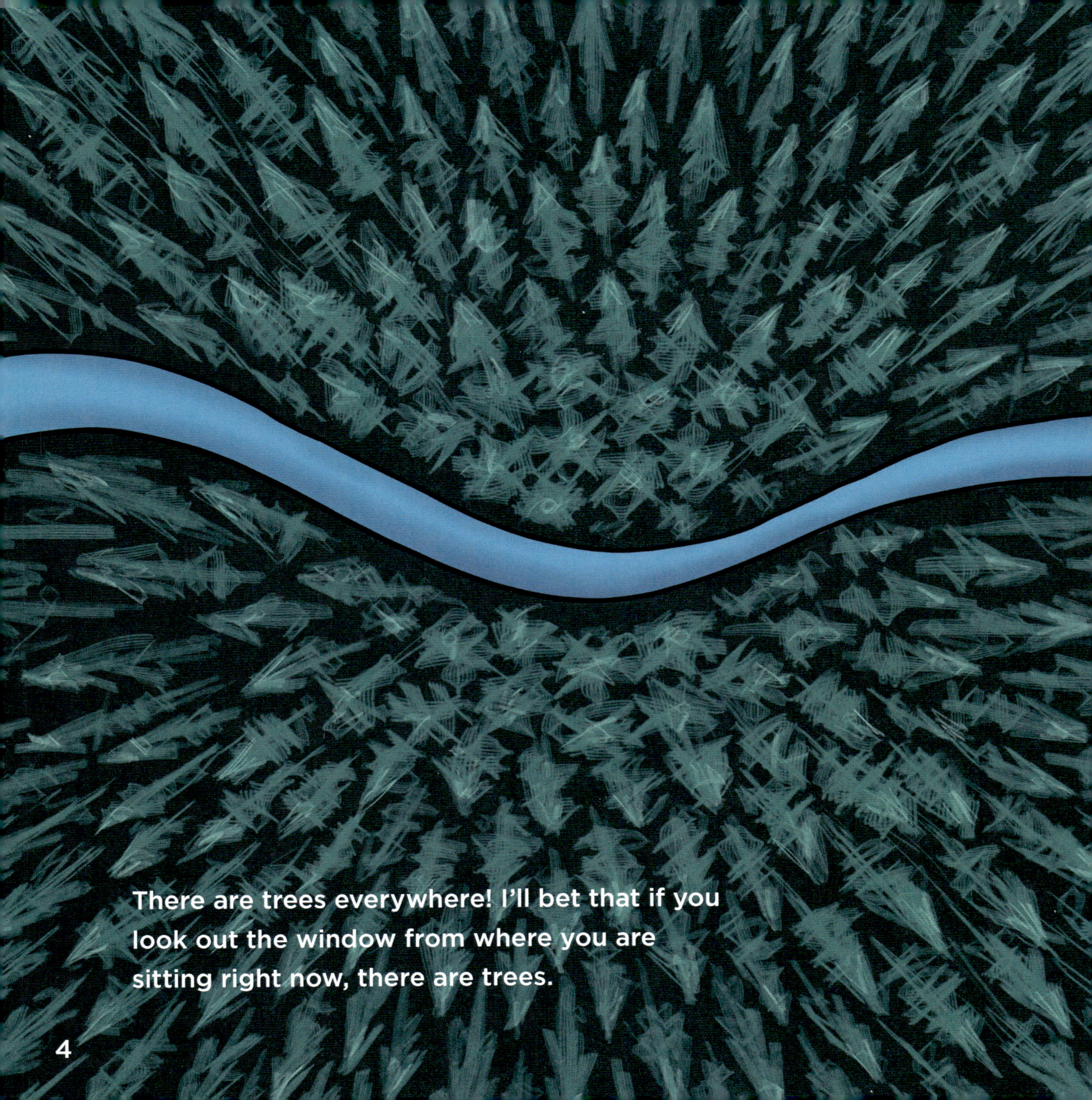

There are trees everywhere! I'll bet that if you look out the window from where you are sitting right now, there are trees.

Go take a look!

Trees have been around since the beginning of time. God planted trees in the Garden of Eden with Adam and Eve to provide beauty and food.

Some trees are green all year long. They are called evergreens. These trees remind us that God is ever-present with us.

He is a faithful God and is always watching over His children. That includes you!

There are lots of different parts to a tree.

Perhaps the most important part of a tree is one that we don't even see because it is hidden underground. It's called the root.

Roots are where the tree takes in water and food to help it grow big and strong. Isn't it interesting that trees get what they need to be healthy from something invisible to us?

The same is true for you and me. Even though our parents feed us the food and drink we need to grow, it is really our invisible God who provides all we need.

This is one reason to say our prayers before meals...

to thank God for giving us what we need to grow!

The roots also keep the tree securely attached to the ground, so that it doesn't fall over whenever there is a storm or strong wind.

In the same way, the Bible says that we need to stay "rooted" in Jesus Christ. He is the one who keeps us strong and stable when the storms of life come.

Did you know that a tree's roots grow stronger when they are tested by storms? We also often become stronger after we experience things that test us or make us sad.

In Matthew 13:3-9, Jesus tells the people a story about different kinds of seeds that became plants. One type of seed became a plant without deep roots. So, when it got very hot from the sun, the plant died because it had no roots to drink water.

Another type of seed had deep roots and grew to be really healthy. This story reminds us always to stay connected to the Lord Jesus. If you do, you will be blessed.

"But the person who trusts in the Lord will be blessed. The Lord will show him that he can be trusted. He will be strong, like a tree planted near water. That tree has large roots that find the water. It is not afraid when the days are hot. Its leaves are always green. It does not worry in a year when no rain comes. That tree always produces fruit."

- Jeremiah 17:7-8

JC LOVES
ME

Above the ground, connected to the roots, is the trunk of the tree. Some trunks are narrow and others are wide. The older the tree gets, the wider it becomes.

You can tell how old a tree is by counting its rings when you cut it down.

Trunks must be strong. They remind us that God is strong. When a tree is cut down, trunks provide wood to build homes, furniture, toys, and other things we use and enjoy. We also use wood to make fires that keep us warm!

God knows what we need. Thats why He made millions and millions of trees. He is our provider!

"...hope in God, who richly provides us with everything for our enjoyment."
- 1 Timothy 6:17

Perhaps the most important thing that the trunk of a tree has ever been used for was to make the cross. The cross is where Jesus hung and died to save us from our sins.

Sin is when we do bad things that deserve punishment. Jesus never sinned, so He did not deserve to be punished. But He loves us so much that He decided to take the punishment that was meant for us. So, let's thank Jesus every day when we say our prayers.

"For God so loved the world that He gave His only begotten Son, that whoever believes in Him should not perish but have everlasting life."

- John 3:16

Connected to the trunk are the branches! At the ends of the branches are the beautiful leaves, flowers, and fruit that we see and love.

Branches almost always point toward the sky in praise to God... like when people raise their hands to God. When the wind blows, they sound like they're clapping and singing, like many people do in church. Try to listen for that the next time it is windy outside.

"You will go out in joy and be led forth in peace; the mountains and hills will burst into song before you, and all the trees of the field will clap their hands."
- Isaiah 55:12

For branches to live, they must be attached to the trunk! Otherwise, they fall to the ground and are not good for much, except to burn in a fire.

In the same way, we need to stay close to the Lord to live lives that will produce beautiful things, just like the flowers and fruit of a tree.

Branches also provide shade, homes for birds in nests, food for squirrels and insects, a playground for monkeys, and a place for us to hang a swing!

The part of the tree that we notice right away is the leaves. God made leaves in all kinds of shapes, but most are broad, flat, and thin.

Leaves are very important. They use light from the sun and water to produce a part of the air that we need to breathe. Maybe that's why God put so many trees on earth… because He loves us and always wants us to have fresh air to breathe!

Do you like being outside when it's windy and rainy? I don't! I try to find a dry, warm place to hide. But leaves are always outside, even in bad weather. They don't complain.

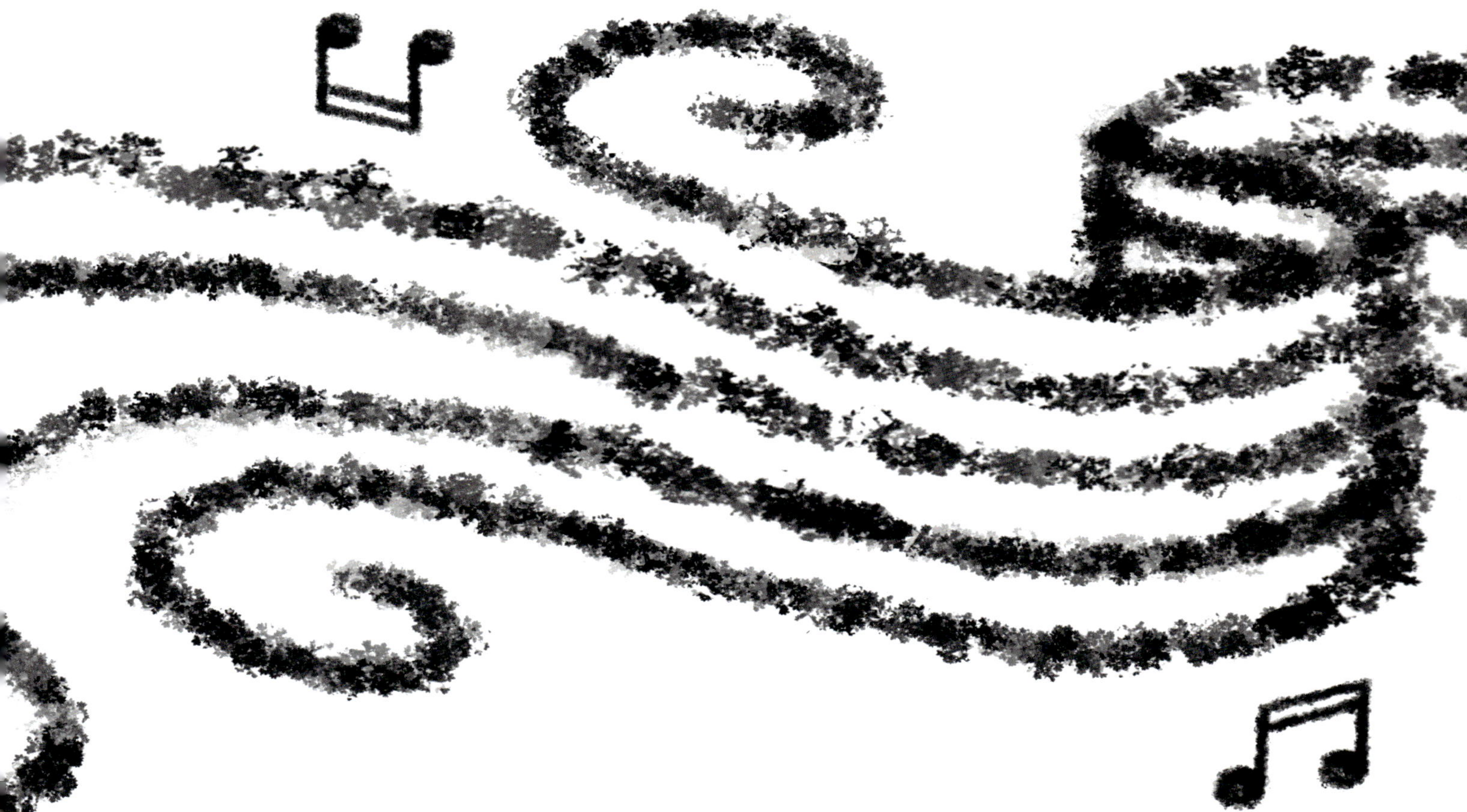

When the wind blows hardest and the rain is strongest and the leaves seem like they're under attack, they often rustle and make music for their Creator! That should remind us that we should sing praises to our King, even when we feel like complaining.

"Do everything without grumbling or arguing."
- Philippians 2:14

In the fall, as leaves prepare to die, many change into pretty colors. Isn't it interesting that when they are near the end of their lives, they are the most beautiful?

Some people are like
that too, like many
of our grandparents.

When leaves and people get older, they are often weaker and eventually die. When the wind blows, leaves are blown off the tree and fall to the ground.

Have you ever noticed, though, that as the leaves fall, they look peaceful? That's a reminder for people who love God and believe in Jesus that there is no fear of death because we are going to live forever with Him in Heaven!

The tree starts out as a seed in the dirt underground. Soon it becomes a small twig and, after many years and many different seasons of life, it becomes a fully grown tree.

We also go through many different seasons in our lifetime.

Some seasons are fresh and beautiful like spring or sunny like summer, but others are dry like fall or cold and dark like winter.

The important thing is to continue to grow in every season. God is faithful and will always provide what we need in each season, no matter what the weather is like.

Trees are all around us, just like God is all around us. Next time you see a tree, remember how much He loves you!

Is it any wonder that God loves trees?

As much as God loves trees, He loves you even more! If you believe in Jesus, you will live with Him forever in Heaven!

“Whoever has ears, let them hear what the Spirit says to the churches. To the one who is victorious, I will give the right to eat from the tree of life, which is in the paradise of God.

- Revelation 2:7”

What have we learned about God through the trees He made?

He is:

- Creative
- Always with us
- Faithful
- Trustworthy
- Strong
- Our Provider
- Our Savior
- Praiseworthy
- King

Upcoming books in the "God Loves..." series:

- God Loves the Ocean
- God Loves Mountains
- God Loves the Moon and the Stars

A native New Yorker, Dr. Vanarthos now resides in Cary, North Carolina with his wife Jill of 27 years. He has two daughters. His oldest, Olivia, is the illustrator of this book! His other daughter, Madalyn, is studying music therapy at Belmont University in Nashville, Tennessee. Dr. Vanarthos is a radiologist, but enjoys writing, reading, Bible study, traveling, and watching New York Giants football in his free time. He has authored a prior book on Christian apologetics titled "What Are the Odds?"

An illustrator and teacher, Olivia strives to encourage young people in their creative thinking. She lives in Quito, Ecuador with her husband and adventure buddy Joshua, where they spend their free time hammocking in the trees, shooting each other with paintballs, and dreaming of far off places.

Made in the USA
San Bernardino, CA
27 January 2020

63663385R00029